FIRST SCIENCE

Matter

by Kay Manolis

POLK SCHOOL
LIBRARY MEDIA CENTER

Consultant:
Duane Quam, M.S. Physics
Chair, Minnesota State
Academic Science Standards
Writing Committee

BLASTOFF! 4 READERS

BELLWETHER MEDIA • MINNEAPOLIS, MN

Note to Librarians, Teachers, and Parents:

Blastoff! Readers are carefully developed by literacy experts and combine standards-based content with developmentally-appropriate text.

Level 1 provides the most support through repetition of high-frequency words, light text, predictable sentence patterns, and strong visual support.

Level 2 offers early readers a bit more challenge through varied simple sentences, increased text load, and less repetition of high frequency words.

Level 3 advances early-fluent readers toward fluency through increased text and concept load, less reliance on visuals, longer sentences, and more literary language.

Level 4 builds reading stamina by providing more text per page, increased use of punctuation, greater variation in sentence patterns, and increasingly challenging vocabulary.

Level 5 encourages children to move from "learning to read" to "reading to learn" by providing even more text, varied writing styles, and less familiar topics.

Whichever book is right for your reader, Blastoff! Readers are the perfect books to build confidence and encourage a love of reading that will last a lifetime!

This edition first published in 2008 by Bellwether Media.

No part of this publication may be reproduced in whole or in part without written permission of the publisher. For information regarding permission, write to Bellwether Media Inc., Attention: Permissions Department, Post Office Box 1C, Minnetonka, MN 55345-9998.

Library of Congress Cataloging-in-Publication Data
Manolis, Kay.
  Matter / by Kay Manolis.
    p. cm. — (Blastoff! readers. First science)
Summary: "First Science explains introductory physical science concepts about matter through real-world observation and simple scientific diagrams. Intended for students in grades three through six"—Provided by publisher.
  Includes bibliographical references and index.
  ISBN-13: 978-1-60014-130-0 (hardcover : alk. paper)
  ISBN-10: 1-60014-130-7 (hardcover : alk. paper)
  1. Matter—Juvenile literature. 2. Matter—Properties—Juvenile literature. I. Title.

  QC173.36.M36 2008
  530—dc22   2007021058

Contents

What Is Matter?

It is a beautiful day at the park! What does everything here have in common? Everything you see is matter. People, rocks, and toys are matter. Water is matter. Everything you can see, touch, taste, or smell is matter.

Even some things you cannot see, touch, taste, or smell are matter. The air is matter. Matter is everything that has **mass** and takes up space as a **gas**, **liquid**, or **solid**.

200 mL
±5%
150
100
50

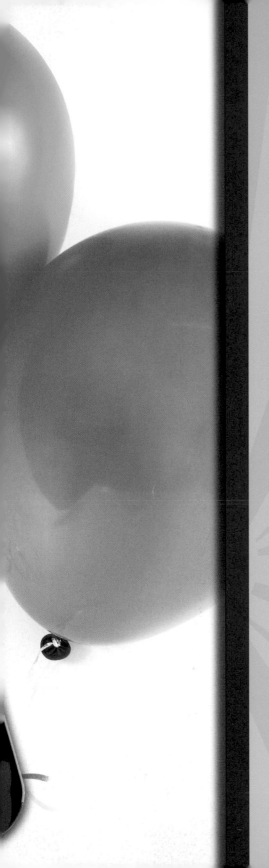

Matter comes in different forms. Some kinds of matter are solids such as animals and rocks. Some kinds of matter are liquids such as water or juice. Other kinds of matter are gases such as air or **steam**. Solids, liquids, and gases are the three most common forms of matter.

Solids

Solid matter is anything with a shape of its own. Some solid matter is small enough to hold in your hand. Other solid matter is large enough to hold you! Solid matter usually keeps its shape. Sometimes you can do something to change the shape of a solid. For example, clay is a solid that can be turned into a new shape.

Liquids

Liquid matter is something you can pour, such as water or milk. Liquid matter does not have its own shape.

A liquid takes the shape of the container holding it. Liquid that spills flows in all directions.

Gases

Gas is a form of matter you can't usually see. The air you breathe is made up of gases.

Gases take up space just like solids and liquids. Think about how air fills the space inside a tire. A tire with no air inside is flat. Most open spaces in the world are actually filled with gas.

Like liquids, gases do not have their own shape. They fill up other shapes. Look at how air fills up these balloons.

Unlike liquids, you cannot pour gases. Gases spread out in every direction. Look at this gas rising out of the earth.

! fun fact

Solid rock can melt if it gets hot enough. Hot, melted rock can flow out of a volcano like a river of fire. It is called lava.

Matter Can Change Its Form

Matter can change from one form to another. Ice has a shape of its own. That makes it a solid. What happens when you heat ice? It turns into water. Turning a solid into a liquid is called **melting**. If you freeze the water, it would turn back into ice!

fun fact
Water is the only natural thing on Earth found in gas, liquid, and solid forms.

When you heat water, it starts to **boil**.
Boiling water turns it into steam, a gas!
Steam can make this teakettle whistle.

Water can change form easily. Other kinds of matter like these rocks are much more difficult to change to another form.

Some kinds of matter are colorful. Others have no color at all. Some matter smells sweet. Other kinds of matter smell bad. Some kinds of matter weigh a lot. Other kinds of matter hardly weigh anything at all.

There are many different kinds of matter. You could never finish describing all the ways matter can look, smell, or feel. Matter is everything, everywhere!

Glossary

boil—to change liquid matter into gas

gas—a form of matter with no definite shape; gas can fill up any space.

liquid—a form of matter with no definite shape; liquid can spill or flow.

mass—the amount of matter something contains

melting—turning solid matter into liquid matter

solid—a form of matter that usually has a definite shape

steam—the gas form of water; water turns to steam when it boils.

To Learn More

AT THE LIBRARY

Mason, Adrienne. *Change It: Solids, Liquids, Gases and You*. Toronto, Ont.: Kids Can, 2006.

Stille, Darlene. *Matter: See It, Touch It, Taste It, Smell It*. Minneapolis, Minn.: Picture Window, 2004.

Weidner Zoehfield, Kathleen. *What is the World Made Of? All About Solids, Liquids, and Gases*. New York: HarperTrophy, 1998.

ON THE WEB

Learning more about matter is as easy as 1, 2, 3.

1. Go to www.factsurfer.com

2. Enter "matter" into search box.

3. Click the "Surf" button and you will see a list of related web sites.

With factsurfer.com, finding more information is just a click away.

Index

The images in this book are reproduced through the courtesy of: VanHart, left front cover, Ljupco Smokovski, right front cover, Eli Mordechai, bottom front cover; Greg Wright, pp. 4-5; Juan Martinez, pp. 6-7; Gina Smith, pp. 8-9; kalulu, pp. 10-11; Dom Cooley/ESPN/Shazamm, pp. 12-13; Mark William Penny, p. 14; mypokcik, p. 15; Sebastian Duda, p. 16; Tiplyashin Anatoly, p. 17; Rick Lord, p. 18; Panoramic Images,/Getty Images, p. 19; Juan Martinez, pp. 20-21